Sparkly Gems

THIS EDITION
Editorial Management by Oriel Square
Produced for DK by WonderLab Group LLC
Jennifer Emmett, Erica Green, Kate Hale, *Founders*

Editors Grace Hill Smith, Libby Romero, Maya Myers, Michaela Weglinski;
Photography Editors Kelley Miller, Annette Kiesow, Nicole DiMella;
Managing Editor Rachel Houghton; **Designers** Project Design Company;
Researcher Michelle Harris; **Copy Editor** Lori Merritt; **Indexer** Connie Binder; **Proofreader** Larry Shea;
Reading Specialist Dr. Jennifer Albro; **Curriculum Specialist** Elaine Larson

Published in the United States by DK Publishing
1745 Broadway, 20th Floor, New York, NY 10019

Copyright © 2023 Dorling Kindersley Limited
DK, a Division of Penguin Random House LLC
23 24 25 26 10 9 8 7 6 5 4 3 2 1
001-334108-Oct/2023

All rights reserved.
Without limiting the rights under the copyright reserved above, no part of this publication may be reproduced, stored in or introduced into a retrieval system, or transmitted, in any form, or by any means (electronic, mechanical, photocopying, recording, or otherwise), without the prior written permission of the copyright owner.
Published in Great Britain by Dorling Kindersley Limited

A catalog record for this book
is available from the Library of Congress.
HC ISBN: 978-0-7440-7508-3
PB ISBN: 978-0-7440-7509-0

DK books are available at special discounts when purchased in bulk for sales promotions, premiums, fundraising, or educational use. For details, contact: DK Publishing Special Markets,
1745 Broadway, 20th Floor, New York, NY 10019
SpecialSales@dk.com

Printed and bound in China

The publisher would like to thank the following for their kind permission to reproduce their images:
a=above; c=center; b=below; l=left; r=right; t=top; b/g=background

123RF.com: Laurent Renault 12bc, Daniel Rnneberg / saastaja 12-13, Vvoennyy 16bc; **Alamy Stock Photo:** Georgy Shafeev / Science Photo Library 11t; **Dorling Kindersley:** Richard Leeney / Holts Gems, Hatton Garden 6bc, 7bl, Ruth Jenkinson / Holts Gems 6bl, 6br, 7bc, 7br, 8br, 9br, 11bc, 15br, 21bl, 21br, 23tl, 23cla, Tim Parmenter / Natural History Museum, London 9bl; **Dreamstime.com:** Amineimo 13br, BY 23cl, Elinal 4-5, Epitavi 8-9, Bjorn Hovdal 13bl, Igor Kaliuzhny 14-15b, Liubomirt 17b, Nastya22 10-11, Bjrn Wylezich 14-15, Rozaliya 11bl, Peter Sobolev 3cb, 23bl, Sutsaiy 20br, Nopadol Uengbunchoo 1b, Jiri Vaclavek 22b, Vladimirdavydov 18br, 23clb; **Getty Images / iStock:** E+ / ilbusca 20-21, Minakryn Ruslan 19crb; **Science Photo Library:** Dorling Kindersley / UIG 10bc; **Shutterstock.com:** Sebastian Janicki 16-17, PK289 19bl, Pesh Siri 18-19

Cover images: *Front:* **Dreamstime.com:** Vector Moon; *Back:* **Dorling Kindersley:** Ruth Jenkinson / Holts Gems cra

All other images © Dorling Kindersley
For more information see: www.dkimages.com

For the curious
www.dk.com

Sparkly Gems

Libby Romero

Look at the crown.
See the pretty stones.
They are gems!
Let's learn about gems.

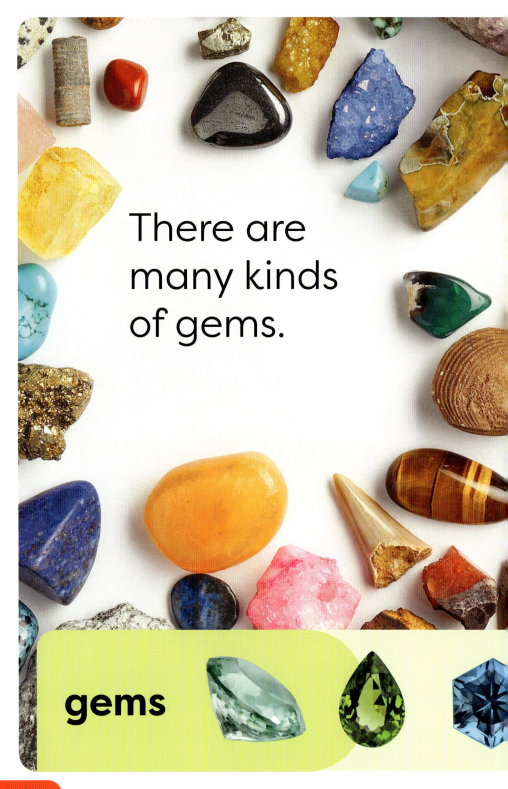

There are many kinds of gems.

gems

They are different colors.

They are different shapes.

Gems are made in different ways.

emeralds

Emeralds are gems. They form deep inside Earth.

Rubies are gems. Some rubies are made in labs.

rubies

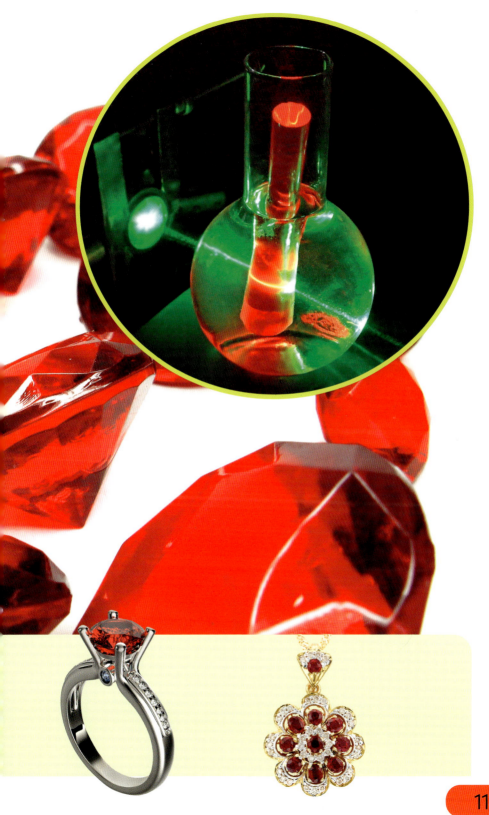

Pearls are gems, too. Oysters make pearls. Oysters are living things!

pearls

Some gems are hard. Diamonds are hard. They are the hardest natural objects on Earth.

diamonds

Other gems are soft.
Fluorite is soft.
It gets scratched.
It breaks easily.

fluorite

black opal

Some gems are rare.
Black opals are rare.
Rare gems are worth
a lot of money.

People cut gems into different shapes. People make gems shine. They use gems to make jewelry.

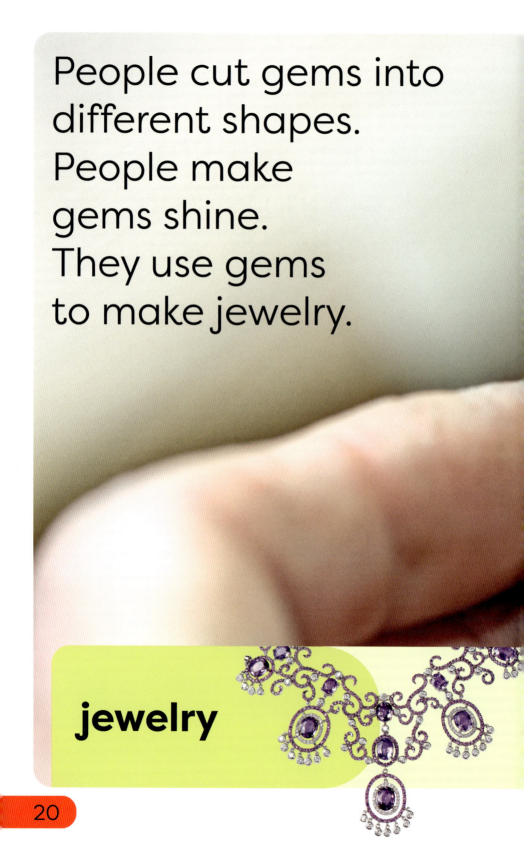

jewelry

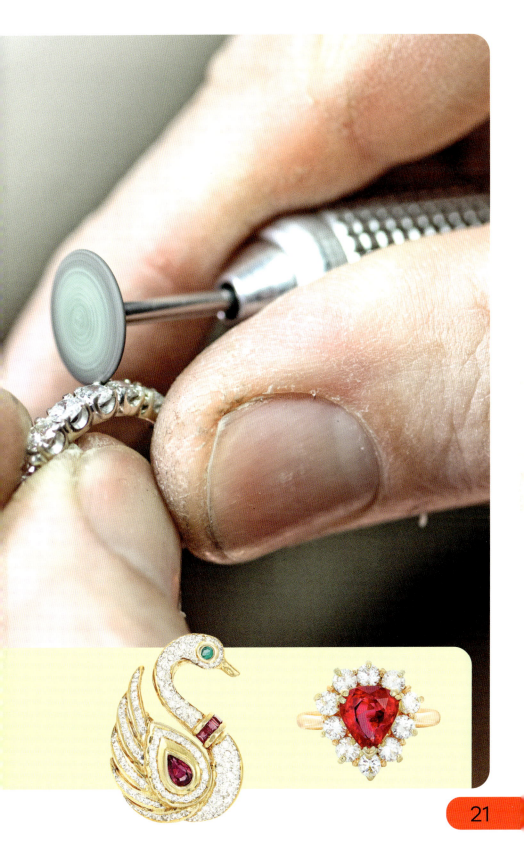

Gems sparkle.
They shine.
They show how beautiful nature can be.

Glossary

gems
beautiful stones that are cut and made smooth to make jewelry

jewelry
fancy items that people wear, like rings, watches, and necklaces

oysters
small ocean animals that make pearls inside their shells

rare
not common

sparkle
to shine with little flashes of light

Quiz

Answer the questions to see what you have learned. Check your answers with an adult.

1. What green gems are made deep inside Earth?
2. Where are some rubies made?
3. What living things make pearls?
4. Why are black opals worth a lot of money?
5. What happens to gems before people use them to make jewelry?

1. Emeralds 2. In labs 3. Oysters 4. They are rare
5. People cut gems into different shapes and make them shine